NATIONAL GEOGRAPHIC | GLOBAL ISSUES

HUMAN RIGHTS

Andrew J. Milson, Ph.D.
Content Consultant
University of Texas at Arlington

Acknowledgments

Grateful acknowledgment is given to the authors, artists, photographers, museums, publishers, and agents for permission to reprint copyrighted material. Every effort has been made to secure the appropriate permission. If any omissions have been made or if corrections are required, please contact the Publisher.

Instructional Consultant: Christopher Johnson, Evanston, Illinois

Teacher Reviewer: Patricia Lewis, Humble Middle School, Humble, Texas

Photographic Credits

Front Cover, Inside Front Cover, Title Page ©Murat Taner/Corbis. **4** (bg) ©Peter Turnley/Corbis. **6** (bg) ©EPA/SERGEY DOLZHENKO/Newscom. **8** (bg) Mapping Specialists. **10** (bg) ©Jon Hicks/Corbis. **13** (bg) ©Marcos Adandia/epa/Newscom. **14** (bg) ©JUAN MABROMATA/AFP/Getty Images. **15** (cl) ©JUAN MABROMATA/AFP/Getty Images. **16** (bg) ©Free Agents Limited/Corbis. **17** (bl) Mapping Specialists. **18** (t) ©Andy Hernandez/Sygma/Corbis. (cr) ©REUTERS/Romeo Ranoco. **20** (bg) ©David Hodges/Alamy. (cl) ©Andy Hernandez/Sygma/Corbis. **22** (bg) ©John Bul Dau. **23** (tl) ©Scott Peterson/Getty Images. **24** (bg) ©NORMAN NG KRT/Newscom. **27** (t) ©MARK RALSTON/AFP/Getty Images/Newscom. **28** (tr) ©Pascal Povani/AFP Creative/Getty Images. **30** (tr) ©NORMAN NG KRT/Newscom. (br) ©Diego Goldberg/Sygma/Corbis. **31** (bg) ©Martin Benik/Westend61/Corbis. (tr) ©Per-Andre Hoffmann/LOOK/Getty Images. (br) ©Pascal Povani/AFP Creative/Getty Images.

MetaMetrics® and the MetaMetrics logo and tagline are trademarks of MetaMetrics, Inc., and are registered in the United States and abroad. The trademarks and names of other companies and products mentioned herein are the property of their respective owners. Copyright © 2010 MetaMetrics, Inc. All rights reserved.

Visit National Geographic Learning online at www.NGSP.com.

Visit our corporate website at www.cengage.com.

Printed in the USA.

RR Donnelley, Menasha, WI

ISBN: 978-07362-97943

13 14 15 16 17 18 19 20 21 22

10 9 8 7 6 5 4 3 2

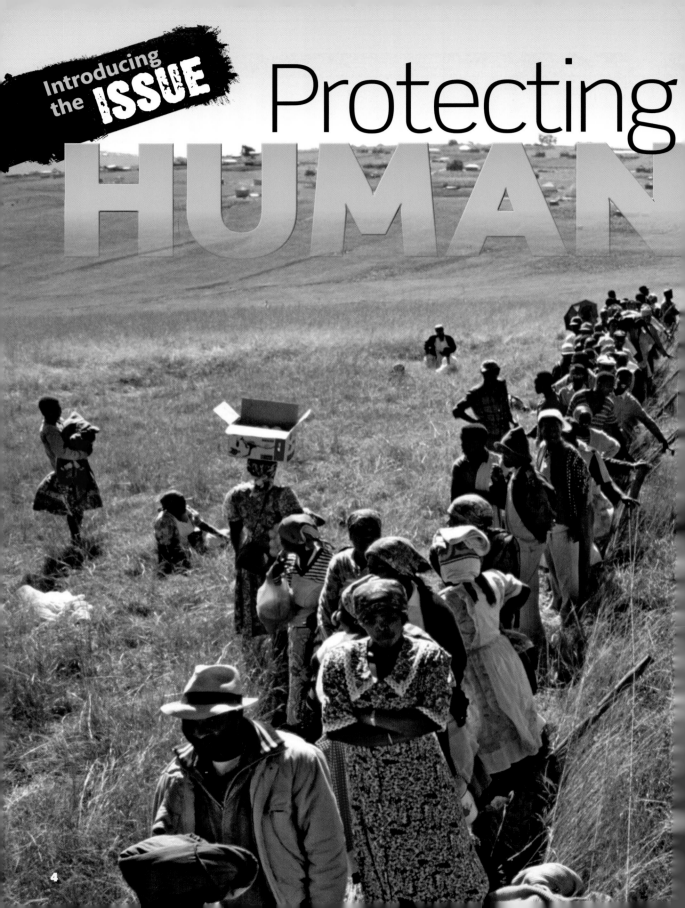

Protecting
HUMAN

RIGHTS

WHAT ARE HUMAN RIGHTS AND HOW DO WE PROTECT THEM?

In April 1994, the world watched in amazement as millions of South Africans waited patiently to vote. Some waited in lines more than a half mile long to choose a president. Why did people take an election so seriously that they would stand in line for hours to vote? South Africans were making history. It was the first time that citizens of all races were allowed to vote in their country. Voting is an important **human right**—a right that every human being should have.

Voters wait to vote in South Africa's first democratic election. The election marked the end of apartheid, an official policy of racial segregation and discrimination against black South Africans.

COMMONLY PROTECTED HUMAN RIGHTS

Right to vote
Freedom from slavery
Freedom of thought
Freedom of religion
Right to own property
Freedom of speech
Freedom of the press
Freedom of assembly
Freedom of movement
Right to a fair trial
Right to equal treatment
    before the law

Source: United Nations Declaration
of Human Rights

Journalists in Ukraine hold signs that read
"Censorship Not!" and "Liberty of Speech."
They are peacefully protesting the government's
attempt to force them off radio and television.
The government has taken this action because
journalists have criticized the government.

THE IMPORTANCE OF HUMAN RIGHTS

The idea of human rights has existed for centuries. Even in ancient Greece, some **philosophers**—people who discuss ideas to gain wisdom—taught that all people have rights. Not even kings could take away people's rights. It was a world-changing idea, but it took almost 2,000 years for governments to begin to respect human rights.

Over time, as democratic institutions developed, the people—not a king or queen—came to be seen as the source of government authority. As a result, some of the earliest laws about human rights safeguarded political rights.

Other commonly protected human rights have been advanced through the years to help people lead full lives. The trend in recent history has been to grant more human rights around the world. Limiting human rights is looked upon as limiting human potential. Human rights matter because they preserve the equality and dignity of people.

KEEPING A WATCHFUL EYE

Human rights are universal, but not all countries protect them, nor do all countries grant exactly the same rights. And even when human rights have been granted, they can be **revoked**, or taken back. This situation can occur when governments are not stable enough to protect human rights. It may also occur when an economic crisis or natural disaster puts pressure on a government. It can happen even in a democracy. For example, in the 1950s, the government of France denied some human rights to people living in Algeria, a North African country that was a French territory at the time.

To prevent such abuses, citizens must work constantly to protect human rights. As you read, you will learn what can happen when people lose their rights. You will also learn how people around the world have fought to regain them.

Explore the Issue

1. **Summarize** What are human rights? Why are they important?

2. **Draw Conclusions** Which rights do you think enable people to take part in the political process?

Human Rights

UNITED STATES The U.S. Constitution guarantees the right to vote, but at first that right didn't apply to women and African Americans. African Americans gained voting rights in 1870. Women gained the right in 1920.

LIBYA In 2011, Libyans publicly protested against their leader, Colonel Mu'ammar al-Qadhafi, who had denied basic rights to Libyans. In October, the rebels captured Qadhafi and began a transition to democracy.

CUBA In 2011, the government of Raúl Castro used arrests, beatings, and forced exile to limit human rights. The authorities punished people who criticized the government.

NORTH AMERICA

NORTH ATLANTIC OCEAN

CASE STUDY 1

ARGENTINA In the 1970s and 1980s, Argentina's government arrested political opponents. Since then, the country has had a democratic government, which recognizes human rights. Officials who violated human rights under the previous government have been arrested.

SOUTH AMERICA

SOUTH PACIFIC OCEAN

SOUTH ATLANTIC OCEAN

Explore the Issue

1. **Find Main Ideas and Details** How does the government of Uzbekistan maintain its control of the country?

2. **Compare and Contrast** Which country has experienced violence associated with elections?

Alert

Study the map below to learn more about human rights situations in countries around the world.

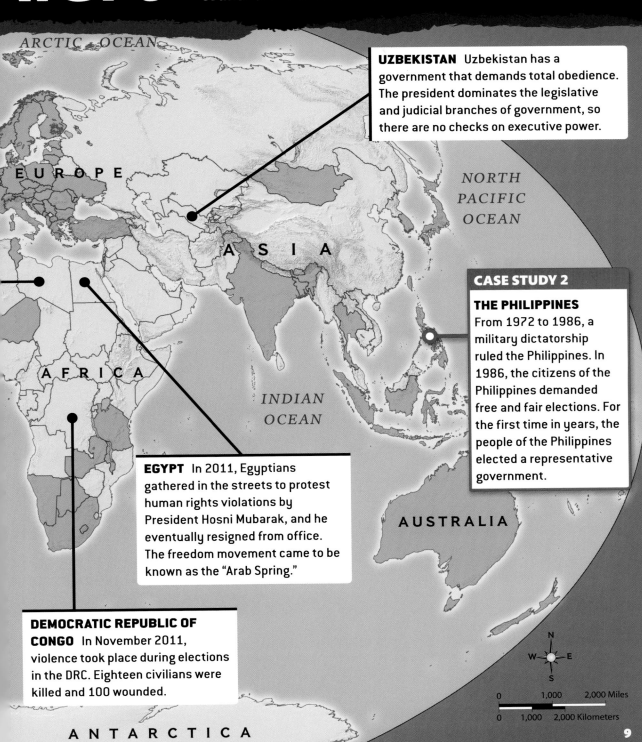

UZBEKISTAN Uzbekistan has a government that demands total obedience. The president dominates the legislative and judicial branches of government, so there are no checks on executive power.

CASE STUDY 2

THE PHILIPPINES
From 1972 to 1986, a military dictatorship ruled the Philippines. In 1986, the citizens of the Philippines demanded free and fair elections. For the first time in years, the people of the Philippines elected a representative government.

EGYPT In 2011, Egyptians gathered in the streets to protest human rights violations by President Hosni Mubarak, and he eventually resigned from office. The freedom movement came to be known as the "Arab Spring."

DEMOCRATIC REPUBLIC OF CONGO In November 2011, violence took place during elections in the DRC. Eighteen civilians were killed and 100 wounded.

ARCTIC OCEAN

EUROPE

ASIA

NORTH PACIFIC OCEAN

AFRICA

INDIAN OCEAN

AUSTRALIA

ANTARCTICA

N
W   E
S

| 0 | 1,000 | 2,000 Miles |
| 0 | 1,000 | 2,000 Kilometers |

Argentina's STRUGGLE for HUMAN RIGHTS

People in the busy city of Buenos Aires, Argentina's capital, now enjoy many freedoms. Not very long ago, residents feared punishment if they spoke out against the government.

WHO AM I?

Francisco Madariaga (mah-dah-RYAH-gah) of Argentina was 32 years old before he met his father. As a child, he was raised by a man named Victor Gallo (GAH-yoh) and his wife. Gallo was an intelligence officer at a secret military prison between 1976 and 1983.

Gallo's job was to get information about enemies of the government. He would force political prisoners to talk about their opposition to the military government that ruled Argentina. When one of those prisoners gave birth to Francisco Madariaga, the authorities took the baby from his mother and gave the infant to the Gallos. They never told Madariaga about his origins. He was raised with the name of Alejandro Ramiro Gallo.

As an adult, Madariaga asked the woman who raised him about his childhood. She admitted that he had been taken from his real mother while she was in prison. Then Madariaga went to a human rights group called Grandmothers of Plaza de Mayo. This organization works to find out what happened to people who disappeared under the military dictatorship. With their help, Madariaga was able to meet his real father, Abel. Describing that milestone, he said, "It was the best moment in my life. I couldn't believe how much I looked like him." According to estimates, Madariaga is far from alone. It is believed that hundreds of children were taken from prisoners and given to members of Argentina's security forces.

What happened to Madariaga and his parents was part of a period in Argentine history known as the Dirty War. During that period, which lasted from 1976 to 1983, the military government seized thousands of people it suspected of being political opponents. Many of those who were arrested were never heard from again. Decades later, Argentina is still coping with some of the results of the Dirty War. It was not until 2010, for example, that Francisco Madariaga met his real father.

In this case study, you will learn what circumstances helped the military government come to power. You will also learn how Argentina continues to recover from this difficult period in its past.

POPULAR APPEAL, LIMITED FREEDOM

Economic troubles often cause countries to turn to **authoritarian**, or strong and controlling, governments. Argentina experienced this effect when a global economic crisis called the Great Depression severely damaged the country's economy. The Great Depression began in 1929. The following year, the military overthrew the elected government.

Continuing economic problems and the tensions of World War II prevented Argentina from developing an effective government. In 1943, the military again overthrew the government. Three years later, Colonel Juan Perón became president. Aided by his popular wife Evita, Perón made changes that helped working people. At the same time, however, he restricted freedoms. After Evita's death in 1952, Perón's popularity faded. Economic growth slowed again. In 1955, the military **exiled** Perón, or sent him out of the country.

THE DIRTY WAR

For nearly 20 years, Argentina wavered between military and civilian rule, though neither solved the country's economic problems. Both revolutionary groups and Perón supporters committed acts of terrorism against the government.

In 1973, Juan Perón became president again with his third wife, Isabel, serving as vice president. When Perón died in 1974, his widow became the world's first woman president of a country. Economic problems continued as prices rose, and unrest spread.

In 1976, the military overthrew Isabel Perón, and the period known as the Dirty War began. A harsh conservative government imposed **censorship**, a ban on publications and broadcasts that criticized the country's leadership. The government also tried to wipe out its opponents. Many of those opponents were activists who believed in social change and more evenly distributing power among all the people in Argentina. Other opponents supported labor unions. The military and secret police arrested thousands of people who protested the government's actions. Many of those people disappeared forever.

The human rights group Grandmothers of Plaza de Mayo gathers in Buenos Aires in 2000. They carry a giant blanket holding the photos of thousands who disappeared during the Dirty War.

The Tower of Babel was created by Argentine artist Marta Minujín to call attention to free speech. It is made up of thousands of books written in languages spoken around the world.

RETURN TO DEMOCRACY

Relatives of the disappeared demanded to know what had happened to their loved ones. Their efforts brought worldwide attention to human rights abuses in Argentina. By the 1980s, the Argentine people were calling for an end to military rule. Then in 1982, the Argentine military invaded but failed to hold some nearby islands ruled by the United Kingdom. This failure increased anger against the military. The next year, Argentina held democratic elections and returned to civilian rule. The new government restored basic political liberties. Political parties could operate freely in Argentina again.

JUSTICE FOR THE DISAPPEARED

The 1980s brought some setbacks for justice in Argentina. Some laws were passed that protected military officers from punishment for past crimes.

Human rights activists continued to demand justice, however. Finally, in 2003, Argentina's Congress overturned the laws that granted **amnesty**, or pardon, to accused officers. Two years later, the country's Supreme Court ruled that those laws were unconstitutional. Since then, more than 50 officials have been convicted of crimes during the Dirty War. Investigations into hundreds of other cases continue.

Since the end of military rule, Argentina's economy has struggled at times. Its democracy, however, has remained stable, with elections described as "generally free and fair" by organizations that monitored them. In this environment, citizens may pursue justice as the country seeks to put the Dirty War behind it for good.

This close-up view shows some of the 30,000 books that make up the tower.

Explore the Issue

1. **Find Main Ideas** How did the military government prevent citizens from exercising their rights?

2. **Analyze Cause and Effect** What people and events brought about the end of the military government?

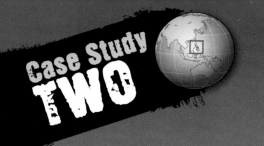
DICTATORSHIP
Democra
IN THE PHILIPPINES

This port is located in Manila, the capital of the Philippines. The country's location and harbors once made it attractive to the conquering Spanish. Sea trade is still important to the Philippines' economy today.

A LAND WITHOUT UNITY

In the Pacific Ocean, east of mainland Southeast Asia, lies an **archipelago**—a group of islands—known as the Philippines. It's a very large group indeed: more than 7,000 islands make up the Philippines. The islands' location and history help explain why the Philippines has been subject to authoritarian rule during its past.

During the Age of Exploration, when Europeans began traveling the world to find new trade routes to the Far East, many ships sailed to Asia from the Americas. The Philippines was located on important European trade routes to Asia. Japan, Korea, China, Vietnam, and Indonesia are all easy to reach from the Philippines. Because of its location, Europeans saw the Philippines as a stepping-stone to important trade locations such as the Spice Islands, a part of Indonesia.

The Philippines differed from most of Southeast Asia in two important ways. First, China and India strongly influenced the rest of Southeast Asia, and their cultures helped unify other countries, but they had little effect on the Philippines.

Secondly, unlike other countries of Southeast Asia, the Philippines never developed its own kingdom. The people who lived in the islands came from many cultures, and they had little contact with one another. Instead of one strong central ruler, many local chiefs governed the Philippines in the 1500s.

This lack of unity made it easier for Spain to conquer the Philippines in the 1500s. The Spanish rulers established a harsh rule over the people of the Philippines, who are known as Filipinos. The Spanish denied the Filipinos human rights for many years. For example, they tried to force the Filipinos to give up their language and religion in favor of Spanish and Catholicism. This heritage of authoritarian rule made it difficult for the Philippines to develop self-government. It also delayed the development of human rights.

Located in the Pacific Ocean, the Philippines is made up of 7,100 islands.

17

THE COLONIAL YEARS

Lack of education was one way the Spanish controlled the country and denied the Filipinos human rights. The Philippines did not have public education until the late 1800s. Instead of educating the Filipinos, the Spanish tried to force most of them to work at growing sugar and hemp for export. The profits benefitted the Spanish. In the 1890s, several revolts against colonial rule occurred.

In 1898, the United States declared war against Spain because of Spanish colonial rule in the Americas. After winning the Spanish-American War, the United States took over Spain's colonies, including the Philippines. The Filipinos hoped for independence, but the United States retained control until the mid-1900s. The United States had military bases there and governed it as a territory. The Philippines did not gain independence until 1946.

Imelda Marcos bought hundreds of pairs of shoes while many Filipinos lived in terrible poverty. The Marikina City Footwear Museum in Metro Manila displays Imelda Marcos's shoe collection.

MARCOS TAKES CONTROL

The newly independent Philippines faced many problems. The islands were recovering from damage suffered during World War II and had a slowly developing economy.

In 1965, Filipinos elected Ferdinand Marcos president; he was reelected in 1969. By law, he could serve only two terms as president, but Marcos wanted to remain in power. To achieve this, he declared **martial law**, or military rule, in 1972.

Marcos violated the people's human rights in many ways. He jailed his political rivals. He ended **habeas corpus**, a law that requires governments to bring charges against people before imprisoning them.

Marcos was able to commit these abuses because he had complete control. The government had no **checks and balances**—a system in which different branches of government share power and keep each other under control.

Corazon Aquino and her running mate Salvador Laurel campaign for the presidential elections in the Philippines.

People flood the streets of Manila to support the ouster of Ferdinand Marcos in 1986.

REESTABLISHING DEMOCRACY

For several years, Marcos ruled without a legislature. People began to resent martial law, and a legislative election was held in 1978. The opposition party, which was led by Benigno Aquino Jr., was popular, but it won no seats. Many people thought Marcos stole the election.

Aquino left the country in 1980. When he returned in 1983, he was immediately assassinated. Anger over his death increased opposition to Marcos. In 1986, Aquino's widow, Corazon Aquino, ran for the presidency. The official results gave the election to Marcos, but again everyone suspected fraud. A revolt occurred, driving Marcos into exile.

Corazon Aquino became president and appointed a commission to write a new constitution, which restored representative government. In addition, she broke up the control Marcos's friends had over the economy.

A ROCKY ROAD

Even though democracy has been restored, the Philippines still faces problems. Poverty remains widespread. The Philippines holds regular elections, but two presidents since Aquino have been charged with corruption. Events such as this undermine people's trust in the government.

Recent presidents have also faced challenges from armed groups that want parts of the Philippines to become independent. President Gloria Arroyo briefly declared martial law in one such region, stirring up memories of Marcos.

On a positive note, Aquino's son Benigno Aquino III was elected president in 2010. During his campaign, he promised to wipe out corruption. If he fulfills that promise, the Philippines will take a giant step toward protecting democracy and human rights.

Explore the Issue

1. **Find Main Ideas and Details** What part of their history made Filipinos used to authoritarian rule?

2. **Draw Conclusions** How do rulers benefit from exerting authoritarian control over a country?

John Bul Dau travels to visit a clinic he helped found in Duk County, South Sudan.

Saving a Lost Generation

THE LOST BOYS OF SUDAN

Lost Boys and others who have fled Sudan stand in a refugee camp in Kenya.

As a boy, National Geographic Emerging Explorer John Bul Dau (BOOL DOW) survived a grueling ordeal. In 1987, during a civil war in Sudan, government troops were sent to attack villages in southern Sudan. Many people feared that the government planned to crush the rebellion by killing all southern males. To survive, thousands of boys fled to neighboring Ethiopia. Twenty thousand escaping children hiked hundreds of miles through wilderness to get there. Soldiers followed them and tried to capture them. The boys faced other difficulties as well. They did not have enough food to eat or water to drink. They suffered from disease, and many of them died along the way. The experience tested the boys' mental strength as well as their physical endurance.

Thirteen-year-old John Bul Dau was one of those **refugees**, people who have fled their country to escape political danger or natural disaster. Dau's group of refugees are now called the Lost Boys of Sudan. Dau was one of the older boys who helped younger children survive. "We chewed tall grasses and ate mud to stay alive," he said. "I was barefoot and wearing no clothes; at night the desert was so cold. We thought about our parents all the time."

TORN BY ETHNIC CONFLICT

When Sudan gained independence from Egyptian and British rule in 1956, it had two distinctly different regions. The north held mostly Arab Muslims. The south held mostly Africans who practiced Christianity or other religions that were common in the region. Independence was granted on the condition that southerners could take part fully in government, but that did not happen. Southerners rebelled, starting a war that lasted from 1983 to 2005.

At the time of the Lost Boys' 1987 trek, the fighting was at its worst. Those who made it alive to Ethiopia stayed in refugee camps for several years. In 1991, political turmoil in Ethiopia caused them to flee again. This time they went to Kenya.

"So many people are still in Sudan needing clinics, schools, and churches. I cannot forget them."—John Dau

The Lost Boys pictured here have been resettled in the United States in Charlotte, North Carolina. They are all from the Dinka tribe in Sudan.

RELOCATION, RECOVERY, REUNION

Dau was one of the boys who made it to Kenya. At the age of 17, he began his education there by learning to write letters and numbers, using a stick to scratch them in the dirt.

A U.S. church decided to bring several of the Lost Boys to the United States. To do so, the church had to agree to **sponsor**, or be responsible for them. Arrangements took some time, and it was 2001 before John Dau reached Syracuse, New York. This young man, who had survived warfare and starvation, was stunned by the abundance in the United States: "On my first trip to the supermarket I couldn't believe there is an entire aisle of food for cats and dogs."

In 2006, the documentary film *God Grew Tired of Us* told the story of his experience. Dau also continued his education, studying public policy at Syracuse University. Just one year earlier, in 2005, a peace agreement had been signed that finally ended the war in Sudan. Amazingly, 20 years after fleeing from his village, Dau was reunited with his family. Now he encourages others not to give up hope.

MAKING A DIFFERENCE

John Dau believes he made it through his ordeal for a purpose. "I feel I survived because God wants to do something with my life. I don't want to waste any of the time I have left. So many people are still in Sudan needing clinics, schools, and churches. I cannot forget them."

Dau has set up two **charitable foundations**, organizations that help people. The John Dau Foundation helps refugees. The South Sudan Institute works for peace, education, and agriculture. Dau also wants to build a health care clinic in South Sudan. John Dau has not forgotten his people nor his promise to help them.

Explore the Issue

1. **Sequence Events** What were the steps in Dau's journey from Sudan to the United States?

2. **Draw Conclusions** What human rights were ignored in this story of the Lost Boys?

What Can I DO?

Conduct a Survey

Find out which rights the First Amendment guarantees. Survey people in your community to discover which of these rights people view as most important. If they had to give up one of those rights, which would they choose and why? Make a presentation that describes your survey results and explains the importance of the right that most would give up.

RESEARCH

- Work in pairs as you use the Internet or library to research the First Amendment in the Bill of Rights.

- Write out the full text of the First Amendment. Look up any words you don't know.

- Make a list of protected rights in the First Amendment.

DISCUSS

- Determine the questions you will ask on your survey.

- Decide whether you will survey other students, adults, or a combination of both groups.

- Select a reasonable number of people to survey. Your survey should represent the people, or a certain group of people, in your community.

In 2010, citizens in California exercised their right to vote guaranteed by the U.S. Constitution.

ANALYZE

- Examine the data. Identify the most important and least important rights based on responses given. Analyze people's reasons as well. Do you notice any patterns?

- Make a graph or chart to organize your data. Be sure to include a title and labels.

- State reasons, facts, and examples to show the importance of the right most would give up.

SHARE

- Make a poster, bulletin, or multimedia presentation to present your results. What conclusions did you draw from your data?

- Conduct a class discussion on this question: Why is it important to protect rights guaranteed by the First Amendment?

- Inspire others to value the First Amendment by discussing instances when these rights have been violated.

Write an Explanatory Article

When the United States was founded, many states kept African Americans and women from voting. Write an article explaining how the United States gradually changed from that system of government to one in which almost all citizens have the right to vote.

RESEARCH

Examine the changes to voting laws that have taken place in the United States since the U.S. Constitution was first adopted. Look for answers to the following questions:

- When was the requirement to own property dropped?
- When and how did women and minorities gain the right to vote? What was the Voting Rights Act of 1965, and why was it important?
- When, how, and why did the voting age change?

Take notes as you research. Select relevant and well-chosen facts, dates, examples, quotations, and concrete details.

DRAFT

Review your notes, organize your information chronologically, and then write your first draft.

- The introductory paragraph should grab the reader's attention. Preview the ideas that will follow by explaining that the right to vote has spread to new groups over time.

- In the body, explain each event that expanded the right to vote. Use a new paragraph for each event, or summarize all the events in one paragraph that uses transitions to signal time.

- In the final paragraph, write a conclusion that follows from and supports the information. Be sure to clarify how the expansion of the right to vote relates to human rights and how it affects democracy.

REVISE & EDIT

Read your first draft. Check that you have used precise language to explain the events that expanded voting rights since the U.S. Constitution was first adopted.

- Does your attention-getting opening relate to the idea of voting rights?

- Have you used transitions to show the relationship between ideas?

- Are the ideas in your middle paragraph(s) organized chronologically? Have you clearly explained how each event gave a new group the right to vote?

- Does your conclusion link voting to the topics of human rights and democracy?

PUBLISH & PRESENT

Now you are ready to publish and present your article. Print out your article or write a clean copy by hand. Add images, graphs, or time lines to help readers understand the information presented. Post your article in your classroom to share with others.

Visual GLOSSARY

amnesty *n.*, official pardon

archipelago *n.*, a group of islands

authoritarian *adj.*, strong and controlling

censorship *n.*, a ban on printed or broadcast material, usually to prevent people from reading opinions the authorities oppose

charitable foundation *n.*, an organization that raises money to help people

checks and balances *n.*, a system in which different branches of government share power and keep each other under control

exile *v.*, to force a person to leave his or her country

habeas corpus *n.*, the requirement that governments must bring charges against people before putting them in prison

human right *n.*, a right that every human being should have

martial law *n.*, rule by the military, often during an emergency

philosopher *n.*, a person who discusses ideas to gain wisdom

refugee *n.*, a person who has fled a country, usually to escape political danger or a natural disaster

revoke *v.*, to take back

sponsor *v.*, to support another person financially or make oneself responsible for that person

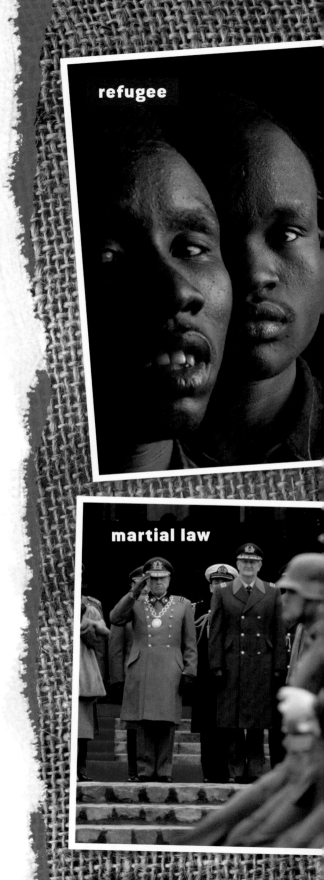

refugee

martial law

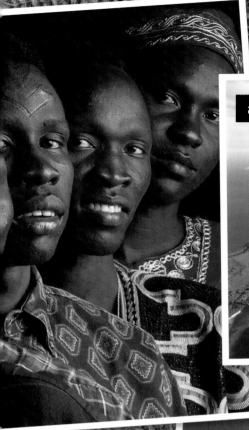

archipelago

human right

INDEX

SKILLS